THE LITTLE BOOK OF

J.R.R. TOLKIEN

Published in 2023 by OH!
An Imprint of Welbeck Non-Fiction Limited, part of Welbeck Publishing Group.

Offices in: London – 20 Mortimer Street, London W1T 3JW
and Sydney – Level 17, 207 Kent St, Sydney NSW 2000 Australia
www.welbeckpublishing.com

ISBN 978-1-80069-374-6

Compiled and written by: Catherine Stephenson
Editorial: Stella Caldwell
Design: Tony Seddon
Project manager: Russell Porter
Production: Jess Brisley

A CIP catalogue record for this book is available from the British Library

Printed in China

10 9 8 7 6 5 4 3 2

THE LITTLE BOOK OF
J.R.R. TOLKIEN

EPIC FANTASY FROM
THE CREATOR OF MIDDLE-EARTH

CONTENTS

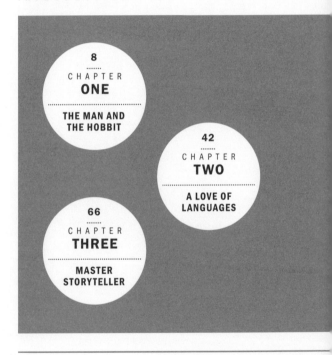

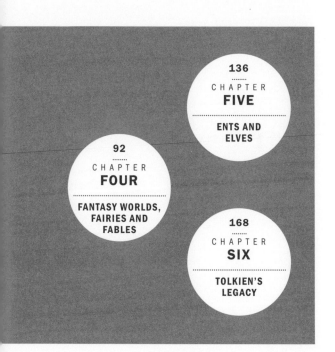

INTRODUCTION

J.R.R. Tolkien was a world-renowned philologist, a professor and, most famously, an inventor of fantasy worlds with magical creatures. That legacy lives on in his epic tales of legend and lore that feature on all-time bestseller lists and in the Hollywood history books too.

To understand Tolkien's extraordinary intellect and imagination, one must return to his younger years. They were marked by loss – of his parents and his boyhood comrades – and his first-hand experience of the horrors of war, but equally by the joys of love, close friendship and learning. He had a profound love of nature, forged in his childhood, an innate affinity for words and a fascination for language.

Tolkien specialized in Old and Middle English and undertook important academic work such as that on *Beowulf*, all of which had a clear influence on his own creations. Devoted to his subject, he loved debating with students or colleagues. But Tolkien had an exceptional imagination and drive, and in his free moments, he would turn to his legendarium: to work on his languages for elves, to bring to life hobbits, orcs, ents, dragons, magicians and giant spiders, and to delicately illustrate maps.

His own invented languages were behind the creation of Middle-earth: as a philologist, he knew that they needed a history in order to survive. This spurred him on to build an entire alternative reality, a believable world with an era-spanning history, and the ultimate epic quest. Drawing from his knowledge of languages, mythology and legend, he brought his greatest passions into his life's work.

Packed with fascinating facts about Tolkien's life and labours, this delightful volume includes quotes from his works, letters and interviews, as well as from his contemporaries and admirers. It's a wonderful celebration of the Oxford professor whose extraordinary imagination and creative genius forever changed the course of fantasy literature.

The Man and the Hobbit

Who was Tolkien? Behind the celebrated scholar, there was a man who cherished the English countryside, a man who had lived through war's horrors and who knew the value of friendship.

He was a Catholic man who met the love of his life at just 16, and a father of four who loved a good debate in a comfy armchair. And he was a man who often said he saw himself as a hobbit...

John Ronald Reuel Tolkien was born in Bloemfontein, South Africa, on 3 January 1892, to British parents.

At the age of three, he returned to Britain with his mother and brother, Hilary, for an extended family visit. But it was to be a one-way journey: while they were away, his father died suddenly in South Africa. Tolkien's mother, Mabel, decided to remain in England.

"I was brought back to my native heath with a memory of something different – hot, dry and barren – and it intensified my love of my own countryside. I could draw you a map of every inch of it. I loved it with an intensity of love that was a kind of nostalgia reversed."

J.R.R. TOLKIEN
Cited by John Ezard in "Tolkien's Shire", *The Guardian*,
28 December 1991

A fluent reader by the age
of four, Tolkien was encouraged to
read widely.

Andrew Lang's *The Red Fairy
Book* was a particular favourite,
especially the story about the
Norse warrior Sigurd, who slew the
dragon Fafnir.

"**D**ragons always attracted me as a mythological element. They seem to be able to comprise human malice and bestiality together so extraordinarily well, and also a sort of malicious wisdom, a shrewdness – terrifying creatures."

J.R.R. TOLKIEN

BBC Radio 4 interview by Dennis Gerrolt, 26 November 1964

Shortly after the death of
Tolkien's father, his mother, Mabel,
converted from non-conformism
to Catholicism. She moved her
family to the hamlet of Sarehole,
near Birmingham, where she initially
homeschooled the children.

The young Tolkien took to country life
like a fish to water.

"I was brought up in considerable poverty, but I was happy running about in that country. I took the idea of the hobbits from the village people and children."

J.R.R. TOLKIEN
Interview with the *Oxford Mail*, 2 August 1966

Tolkien was a staunch Catholic – his faith was no doubt closely bound up with his love for his mother. When he lived and worked in Oxford, he would cycle to early-morning mass every day.

Although he didn't set out to make *The Lord of the Rings* a religious work, theological themes naturally emerged, such as good versus evil, humility triumphing over greed, death and resurrection, and compassion and healing.

"**M**yth and fairy-story, as all art, reflect and contain in solution elements of moral and religious truth (or error), but not explicit[ly]."

J.R.R. TOLKIEN

In a letter to his publisher Milton Waldman in 1951, cited by Jane Chance in *Tolkien's Art: A Mythology for England*, 2001

As a young child in Africa, Tolkien was bitten by a tarantula in the garden. He ran to his nurse, who sucked out the poison.

Although he later claimed the incident left him with no particular dislike of spiders, it's tempting to believe it inspired the monstrous spiders that appear in his stories.

At the age of eight, Tolkien passed the entrance exams for Birmingham's King Edward's School, four miles from Sarehole.

His mother couldn't afford the train fare, so she regretfully gave up the family's much-loved cottage and moved to the city centre.

When Tolkien was 12, his mother, Mabel, died of diabetes, which was, at that time, an untreatable illness. He and his brother, Hilary, were made wards of the parish priest, the half-Spanish, half-Welsh Father Francis Morgan, who would become the boys' "second father".

They lived with aunts and in boarding houses thereafter.

At King Edward's School, the TCBS – Tea Club, Barrovian Society – was founded by Tolkien and his friends Robert Gilson, Geoffrey Smith and Christopher Wiseman.

They shared a knowledge of classical literature and their interests ranged from Renaissance painting to the natural sciences, music and English literature. Tragically, only Tolkien and Christopher would survive the First World War.

Tolkien consistently identified himself as a hobbit. Certainly, he shared with his creatures a love and respect for the natural world around him.

"**I** am in fact a hobbit (in all but size).
I like gardens, trees and unmechanized
farmlands; I smoke a pipe, and like good
plain food (unrefrigerated), but detest
French cooking; I like, and even dare to wear
in these dull days, ornamental waistcoats.
I am fond of mushrooms (out of a field); have
a very simple sense of humour (which even
my appreciative critics find tiresome); I go
to bed late and get up late."

J.R.R. TOLKIEN

In a letter to Deborah Webster, 25 October 1958, cited by
Ralph Wood in *The Gospel According to Tolkien*, 2003

Tolkien had a zest for life and a deep sense of humour. He found amusement in rough and tumble with his children and loved to play practical jokes. He once dressed up as an Anglo-Saxon warrior and chased his astonished neighbour down the street.

As an older man, he was known to hand unsuspecting shopkeepers his false teeth in a pile of change.

"Carriages at midnight

Ambulances at 2 a.m.

Wheelbarrows at 5 a.m.

Hearses at daybreak."

At the foot of an invitation from Tolkien and his wife, Edith,
to celebrate their son Christopher's 21st birthday

Tolkien studied English Language and Literature at Exeter College, Oxford. He had not yet completed his undergraduate studies when England declared war on Germany – though he was able to defer his call-up until after graduation.

In June 1915, he obtained a first-class degree, before hurriedly enlisting in the army. In his stories, Tolkien laments the waste of war that he experienced first hand.

"**T**he world is full enough of hurts and mischances without wars to multiply them."

THE RETURN OF THE KING, 1955

After enlisting in the Lancashire Fusiliers, Tolkien was posted to the Western Front in June 1915 for the start of the Somme offensive – the bloodiest battle of the First World War.

By October, he had contracted trench fever and was sent home. He was devastated by the loss of dear friends and deeply scarred by the atrocities he witnessed.

"**T**hey lie in all the pools, pale faces, deep deep under the dark water. I saw them: grim faces and evil, and noble faces and sad. Many faces proud and fair, and weeds in their silver hair. But all foul, all rotting, all dead."

THE TWO TOWERS, 1954

From "The Dead Marshes", which are reminiscent of the horror of the First World War trenches

When he was just 16, Tolkien met Edith Bratt, three years his senior and another orphan at the boarding house. After a year of shared walks and conversations, the two fell in love.

Concerned at the age gap and her Protestant faith, Father Francis Morgan banned Tolkien from seeing Edith until he was 21. Tolkien obeyed his guardian, but he never forgot Edith. On the eve of his 21st birthday, he wrote to her and the pair were married in March 1916.

"**L**o! young we are and yet have stood like planted hearts in the great Sun of Love so long (as two fair trees in woodland or in open dale stand utterly entwined, and breathe the airs, and suck the very light together) that we have become as one, deep-rooted in the soil of Life, and tangled in sweet growth."

J.R.R. TOLKIEN

Love poem for Edith, cited in Humphrey Carpenter,
J.R.R. Tolkien: A Biography, p. 80, 1977

Tolkien and Edith had four children
together – John, Michael, Christopher
and Priscilla – and remained a close
and devoted couple until Edith's death in
1971, at the age of 82.

"**O**ur goodnights when sometimes you were in your little white nightgown, and our absurd long window talks; and how we watched the sun come up over town through the mist and Big Ben toll hour after hour, and the moths almost used to frighten you away – and our whistle-call – and our cycle-rides – and the fire talks – and the three great kisses."

J.R.R. TOLKIEN

In a letter to Edith, recalling their youthful love, cited in Joseph Pearce, *Tolkien: Man and Myth: A Literary Life*, 2001

Tolkien was an Anglo-Saxon scholar
and philologist.

A philologist studies the history of
language, its grammar and its meaning
by analyzing written texts and oral
traditions of storytelling. It comes from the
Greek word *philologia*, "love of learning,
discussion and literature".

"I am a philologist, and all my work is philological. I avoid hobbies because I am a very serious person and cannot distinguish between private amusement and duty. I am affable, but unsociable. I only work for private amusement, since I find my duties privately amusing."

J.R.R. TOLKIEN

Cited in Harvey Breit, "Oxford Calling",
New York Times Book Review, 5 June 1955

Tolkien spent the vast majority of his life in Oxford. In 1925, he was appointed Rawlinson and Bosworth Professor of Anglo-Saxon at Oxford and stayed in the post for 20 years.

He subsequently became Merton Professor of English Language and Literature, also at Oxford, until his retirement in 1959.

"**I**f you imagine the archetype of the Oxford don ... a little offputting and at a distance, until you got to know him, and then he became immensely warm. Fame puzzled him. He was not pretentious. He lived in a very simple way, wrapped up in his family and own internal world. He laughed a lot and smoked his pipe a lot."

RAYNER UNWIN

Tolkien's publisher describing Tolkien. Cited in
Herbert Mitgang, "Behind the Best Sellers: J.R.R. Tolkien",
New York Times, 2 October 1977

At Oxford, Tolkien struck up a friendship with C.S. Lewis, who shared his love for mythical tales. They began to meet regularly in Lewis's rooms at Magdalen College, and would often talk into the night, commenting on each other's poetry or discussing the Norse gods and giants of Asgard.

This friendship would last a lifetime and be instrumental in both their literary careers.

"**S**o far I have felt the normal feelings of a man of my age – like an old tree that is losing all its leaves one by one: this feels like an axe-blow near the roots."

J.R.R. TOLKIEN

Describing his loss after the death of C.S. Lewis,
in a letter to his daughter, Priscilla, 26 November 1963,
cited in "How C.S. Lewis Helped Encourage Tolkien's
'Lord of the Rings'", *Newsweek*, 3 April 2017

Tolkien's Middle-earth contains a strong theme of environmentalism. The author was extremely sensitive to the encroachments on the English countryside he so loved.

In his Middle-earth, Tolkien describes the devastating impact of industrialization at Isengard and in Mordor: the inhabitants are orcs, goblins and uruk-hai, and the landscape is dark, rocky and stony, with wastelands full of machinery and fortresses used for destruction.

"**T**here is always a smoke rising from Isengard these days. 'Curse him, root and branch! Many of those trees were my friends, creatures I had known from nut and acorn; many had voices of their own that are lost for ever now. And there are wastes of stump and bramble where once there were singing groves."

TREEBEARD

The oldest of Middle-earth's ents tells Merry and Pippin how the orcs have come to destroy the trees, *The Twin Towers*, 1954

CHAPTER
TWO
A Love of Languages

Language is at the very core of who Tolkien was. Not only was he a brilliant linguist who effortlessly mastered both modern and ancient languages, but he had an innate fascination and flair for language that drove both his scholarship and his writing.

Tolkien had an unusual sensitivity to the sound and appearance of words.

His interest was piqued as a child when he saw Welsh words on coal trucks travelling to and from South Wales, with destination names like "Nantyglo", "Penrhiwceiber" and "Senghenydd".

"**B**ut all the time there had been another call ... It struck at me in the names on coal-trucks; and drawing nearer, it flickered past on station-signs, a flash of strange spelling and a hint of a language old and yet alive; even in an *adeiladwyd* [built] 1887, ill-cut on a stone-slab, it pierced my linguistic heart.

J.R.R. TOLKIEN

The Monsters and the Critics: And Other Essays, 1983

For most of his career, Tolkien taught Old English, Middle English and the history of the English language.

Much of the poetry and prose of Anglo-Saxon and early medieval England was written in the West Midlands dialect that had been spoken by his mother's ancestors, and he felt a great personal link to it.

" **I** am a West-midlander by blood, and took
to early West-midland Middle English as to a
known tongue as soon as I set eyes on it."

J.R.R. TOLKIEN

In a letter to the poet W.H. Auden, 7 June 1955, cited on the
Tolkien Estate website www.tolkienestate.com

In 1916, while hospitalized with trench fever, Tolkien set to work writing his first Elvish word-list, as well as the first fragments of what would become *The Silmarillion*.

In fact, the two were intimately related – the writer's invented languages were the basis for everything else, and he made up his stories to create a world for them, rather than the other way round.

"**T**he making of language and mythology are related functions ... Your language construction will breed a mythology."

J.R.R. TOLKIEN

From his 1930s essay "A Secret Vice",
first published in
The Monsters and the Critics and Other Essays, 1983

As a lecturer, Tolkien delighted in sharing his passion for his subject area with his students.

He began his lecture series on *Beowulf* by loudly reciting the opening lines of the poem in the original Anglo-Saxon, with a great cry of *"Hwæt!"*

"**A**t a time when it was distinctly unfashionable for undergraduates to be enthusiastic about anything, a Tolkien lecture received a standing ovation; as one student said, with Tolkien you were in the meadhall; he was the bard, you were the drinking, listening guests."

WILLIAM CATER

Cited in "More and More People are Getting the J.R.R. Tolkien Habit", *Los Angeles Times*, 9 April 1972

In 1920, Tolkien was appointed Reader in English Language at the University of Leeds. He found a friend as well as a colleague in fellow professor Eric Gordon, with whom he shared a love of medieval philology.

They worked together, most notably on an edition of the 14th-century Middle-English chivalric romance *Sir Gawain and the Green Knight*.

At Leeds, Tolkien and Eric Gordon founded a "Viking Club" for philologists and historians specializing in Germanic and Scandinavian studies, who would gather to read sagas.

They also made up rude verses about the students, sang drinking songs in Old Norse, translated nursery rhymes into Anglo-Saxon, and, of course, drank lots of beer.

Tolkien thought that all languages were intrinsically either attractive or repulsive.

He found Welsh a language of intrinsic beauty.

"**M**ost English-speaking people, for instance, will admit that cellar door is "beautiful", especially if dissociated from its sense (and its spelling). More beautiful than, say, sky, and far more beautiful than beautiful. Well then, in Welsh for me cellar doors are extraordinarily frequent."

J.R.R. TOLKIEN

From "English and Welsh", a speech for the O'Donnell Lectures at the University of Oxford, 21 October 1955. Included in Christopher Tolkien (ed.), *The Monsters and the Critics and Other Essays*, 1983

Tolkien was an inventor of languages. Over his lifetime, he developed his initial "nonsense fairy language" – which would eventually become the tongue of his elves – into a body of interrelated languages with a complex history.

He mapped these out in "The Tree of Tongues" sketch, published in 1987 in *The Lost Road and Other Writings*.

"I wish life was not so short. Languages take such a time, and so do all the things one wants to know about."

ALBOIN ERROL

From Tolkien's 1920 unfinished story "Lost Road", later published in *The Lost Road and Other Writings*, 1987

From 1919 to 1920, Tolkien worked as a lexicographer for the *Oxford English Dictionary*. He was assigned to the "W"s, charged with explaining the origins and development of words like *warm*, *wasp*, *wain* and *waggle* in a dictionary entry.

His background and philological training made him the ideal candidate for the work.

"His work gives evidence of an unusually thorough mastery of Anglo-Saxon and of the facts and principles of the comparative grammar of the Germanic languages. Indeed, I have no hesitation in saying that I have never known a man of his age who was in these respects his equal."

DR HENRY BRADLEY

Tolkien's supervisor when he worked on the
Oxford English Dictionary. Cited in Humphrey Carpenter,
J.R.R. Tolkien: A Biography, 1977

After Tolkien discovered his two great language loves, Welsh and Finnish, they became the main influences on his own linguistic constructions.

He wanted his Elvish tongues to be European in style and structure but also aesthetically pleasing.

"*E*len síla lúmenn' omentieimo"
['A star shines on the hour of our meeting']"

FRODO

A Quenya greeting used by Frodo in
The Fellowship of the Ring, 1954

Tolkien's invented languages had their own history within Middle-earth.

The Elvish languages Quenya and Sindarin (High-elven or Grey-elven) developed from a common, prehistoric Eldarin tongue, just like English, German, French or Spanish are descended from a common ancestor.

All of the Elvish poems, songs, exclamations, spells and invocations in *The Hobbit*, *The Lord of the Rings* and *The Children of Húrin* are in Quenya and Sindarin.

The Black Speech, also known as the
Dark Tongue of Mordor, is one of the
fictional languages constructed by Tolkien
for his legendarium. Sauron created it as
a common tongue for all the servants of
Mordor, which was spoken alongside
other languages like Orkish.

The harsh vowels and clusters of
consonants and jagged sounds lend
themselves to a coarse and harsh
pronunciation, so much so that Tolkien
himself found the language distasteful
and did not enjoy writing in it.

The only example of pure Black Speech is the inscription on the One Ring.

"Ash nazg durbatulûk, ash nazg gimbatul, ash nazg thrakatulûk agh burzum-ishi krimpatul."

This translates as, "One Ring to rule them all, One Ring to find them, One Ring to bring them all and in the Darkness bind them."

CHAPTER
THREE

Master Storyteller

Tolkien began telling and writing stories as a child, and continued to do so as he grew up. However, he never set out to be a novelist – he was focused on his responsibilities at Oxford and on raising his family.

Rather, he was driven to write through his love of language, its roots and its history.

Tolkien's scholarly publications were relatively few in number, but often extremely influential.

His paper "Beowulf, the Monsters and the Critics" (1936) was a turning point in studies of *Beowulf*, the oldest-surviving epic poem in English.

In it, he defends the poem's fantastical nature, arguing that it conveys a surprisingly universal and atemporal world view.

"It is just because the main foes in *Beowulf* are inhuman that the story is larger and more significant than this imaginary poem of a great king's fall. It glimpses the cosmic and moves with the thought of all men concerning the fate of human life and efforts; it stands amid but above the petty wars of princes, and surpasses the dates and limits of historical periods, however important."

Beowulf, the Monsters and the Critics, 1936

The Father Christmas letters were written and illustrated by Tolkien, for his children, between 1920 and 1943. Each Christmas, they came through the letterbox – complete with North Pole stamps and postage marks as designed by Tolkien – and related the adventures and misadventures of Father Christmas and his helpers.

In the letter opposite, Father Christmas describes how his polar-bear helper is more hindrance than help.

"It all happened like this: one very windy day last November my hood blew off and went and stuck on the top of the North Pole. I told him not to, but the N.P. Bear climbed up to the thin top to get it down – and he did."

J.R.R. TOLKIEN

From "Xmas 1925" in *Letters From Father Christmas*, 1976

Tolkien was one of the founders of "The Inklings", an informal literary discussion group in Oxford.

The members – including C.S. Lewis, who was one of Tolkien's closest friends, Charles Williams and Owen Barfield – met regularly for drinks, readings and discussions of their work.

Tolkien never missed a chance to make up stories to amuse his family.

Inspired by signs hanging on local gates in Oxford saying "Bill Stickers Will Be Prosecuted", Tolkien created a villain called "Bill Stickers" who always got away with everything, and his nemesis "Major Road Ahead", who was always in his pursuit.

The tale at the heart of *The Silmarillion* – that of Beren, a mortal man, who loves Lúthien Tinúviel, an elven-maid and immortal – was inspired by Tolkien's love for his wife, Edith.

The author described how, on a walk together, Edith sang and danced for him in a small wood with an undergrowth of hemlock, just as Beren falls in love when he sees Lúthien singing and dancing in a glade in the moonlight. Thus, Tolkien came to think of Edith as "Lúthien" and himself as "Beren".

Tolkien had the name "Luthien" engraved on his wife Edith's headstone. When he died in 1973, he was buried in the same grave with the name "Beren" added to the memorial. Before his death, he wrote to his son Christopher:

"**F**or she was (and knew she was) my Luthien."

J.R.R. TOLKIEN

Cited on the Tolkien Estate website www.tolkienestate.com

The inspiration for *The Hobbit* came to Tolkien unexpectedly in the summer of 1930. As he wearily worked his way through a huge stack of student essays, the idea seemed to pop into his head from nowhere.

"On a blank leaf I scrawled: 'In a hole in the ground there lived a hobbit.' I did not and do not know why."

J.R.R. TOLKIEN

Describing the origins of *The Hobbit* in a letter to
the poet W.H. Auden, 7 June 1955, cited in David Day,
The Hobbit Companion, 2012

The Hobbit was initially for Tolkien's personal amusement. He certainly didn't intend to link it to his work in *The Silmarillion* – although, over time, he drew in elements of his mythology. Even so, it was essentially a children's story, and since Tolkien's children had become too old to be read to, the almost-finished manuscript just sat there.

It would take a twist of fate for *The Hobbit* to be shared with the world.

"Tolkien let a few of his Oxford friends read *The Hobbit*. One, a tutor, lent it to a student, Susan Dagnell. When, some time later, Miss Dagnell joined Allen & Unwin, the publishers, she suggested it as a children's book."

C. PLIMMER & D. PLIMMER

From "The Man Who Understands Hobbits." *London Daily Telegraph Magazine*, 22 March 1968

Tolkien's stories are full of verses,
chants and rhymes. Some provide
historical and cultural details about
Middle-earth or draw a picture
of the singers.

The chant of the goblins when they
first capture Bilbo and the dwarves
conveys their cruel and violent nature.

"**C**lap! Snap! the black crack!
Grip, grab! Pinch, nab!"

THE HOBBIT, 1937

Sung by the Goblins when they capture Bilbo Baggins,
Thorin and the other dwarves

The Silmarillion was Tolkien's ultimate labour of love. It is the history of Middle-earth, from the creation of the universe to the end of the Third Age. Conceived during the First World War, Tolkien worked on the book throughout his life.

It was posthumously edited and published by his son Christopher in 1977, making it both precursor of and sequel to *The Lord of the Rings*.

TOP 10 MIDDLE-EARTH BOOKS

The Lord of the Rings

The Hobbit

The Children of Húrin

Master of Middle-earth: The Fiction
of J.R.R. Tolkien's Middle-earth

The Silmarillion

Unfinished Tales of Numenor and
Middle-earth

The Adventures of Tom Bombadil

Morgoth's Ring

The War of the Jewels

The People of Middle-earth

The short story *Leaf by Niggle* (written between 1938 and 1939) reflects Tolkien's own creative process, and, to some extent, his life.

Like the painter in his story who "niggled" over the details of every leaf of the tree, Tolkien knew he would finish *The Lord of the Rings* to perfection, or not at all.

"**H**e used to spend a long time on a single leaf, trying to catch its shape, and its sheen, and the glistening of dewdrops on its edges. Yet he wanted to paint a huge tree."

LEAF BY NIGGLE

First published in the *Dublin Review*, January 1945

The Hobbit and *The Lord of the Rings* were born of the fruit of Tolkien's dedication to his legendarium: the mythology and historical setting, the elvish languages, even an alphabet, Fëanorian, which he used for elvish inscriptions.

As for the hobbits, they just appeared one day.

"**L**ong before I wrote *The Hobbit* ... I had constructed this world mythology ... I got sucked into it as the hobbit did itself. As you know, *The Hobbit* was originally about these dwarves and as soon he got moving out into the world he got moving and slipped into it."

J.R.R. TOLKIEN

BBC Radio 4 interview by Dennis Gerrolt, 26 November 1964

Tolkien set out to write a sequel to *The Hobbit* in 1937. *The Lord of the Rings* was finally published in 1954–55. The author wrote when he had the time, sometimes with long breaks, and produced numerous drafts.

In 1949, Tolkien had penned the last page to his book. But then there was a great deal of revision to be done ... and typing.

"**T**here was a tremendous lot of revision.
I typed the whole of that work out twice and
lots of it, many times, on a bed in an attic.
I couldn't afford, of course, the typing."

J.R.R. TOLKIEN
BBC Radio 4 interview by Dennis Gerrolt, 26 November 1964

**THE LORD OF THE RINGS
IN NUMBERS**

12 years to write

5 years to be published

3 volumes, 1,178 pages,
around half a million words

More than 150 million
copies sold

Translated into more than
38 languages

"The Road Goes Ever On" is a song cycle comprising several walking songs in *The Hobbit* and *The Lord of the Rings*.

It certainly did go on for Frodo Baggins and Samwise Gamgee, who walked somewhere in the realm of 1,400 miles (2,253 km) to get from Bag End to Mount Doom.

Fantasy Worlds, Fairies and Fables

In Middle-earth, Tolkien created a rich and believable world, complete with history and detail.

Drawing from the myths and legends of Europe's medieval past, he built a new universe – as complex and vivid as the real world, but so much more exciting.

By transforming the traditional fairy tale
and reintroducing it to a new audience,
Tolkien, in a sense, created a new genre.

A key feature of this was the addition
of a map to the fantasy novel. Tolkien's
maps were special in that they had
a consistent history and geography, and
were created to give the feeling they
were indefinitely extendable.

"**W**hen Tolkien drew his maps and covered them with names, he felt no need to bring all the names into the story. They do their work by suggesting that there is a world outside the story ... Middle-earth is different from its many imitators in its density, its redundancy, and consequently its depth..."

TOM SHIPPEY

From *J.R.R. Tolkien: Author of the Century*, 2000

secondary world

A term used by Tolkien to refer to a consistent, fictional world or setting, with its own internal logic, laws and systems, and several inter-dependent dimensions, such as geography, characters, languages and timeline, all aimed at providing a completely convincing picture so that people could "get inside the story".

As recently as 2015, a map of Middle-earth annotated by Tolkien himself was discovered tucked away inside a copy of *The Lord of the Rings*.

According to this, Hobbiton is on the same latitude as Oxford, and the Italian city of Ravenna could be the inspiration behind the fictional city of Minas Tirith.

"Middle-earth" is equivalent to
the *Miðgarðr* of Norse mythology and
Middangeard in Old English works,
including *Beowulf*.

It is the main continent of Earth *(Arda)*
in an imaginary historical period,
ending with Tolkien's Third Age, about
6,000 years ago.

"**M**iddle-earth is the whole of the inhabitable parts of the world: this world. I used it because in your putting over mythological stuff of that kind, it's desirable if you can ... use words that are already in existence – which have a certain sense ... And therefore I use 'dwarves', and 'Middle-earth', and 'elves' and so on. You can't have everything absolutely strange at the outset."

J.R.R. TOLKIEN

Tolkien in Oxford, a BBC2 television documentary featuring an interview with Tolkien by John Izzard, 1968

"If you really want to know what Middle-earth is based on, it's my wonder and delight in the earth as it is, particularly the natural earth."

J.R.R. TOLKIEN
Cited in "J.R.R. Tolkien Dead at 81; Wrote 'Lord of the Rings'",
New York Times, 3 September 1973

At Oxford, Tolkien founded a group called The Coalbiters or *Kolbitars*, who gathered to read Old Icelandic adventures and sagas.

Coalbiters are a type of character or a genre in the Old Norse period, in which a young man who lounges by the fire insead of working is roused to act and unexpectedly becomes the protagonist in a saga – much like Bilbo Baggins, Frodo or Sam.

Tolkien's tales of Middle-earth are mostly set in on the north-west of the continent, which is suggestive of Europe.

The landscapes of the Shire are reminiscent of England, particularly the West Midlands. The years the author spent there as a young child clearly gave him a lasting attachment to the area.

"I was born in Bloomsdale in South Africa ... then, to have just at the age when imagination is opening out, suddenly find yourself in a quiet Warwickshire village, I think it engenders a particular love of what you might call central Midlands English countryside. Based on good water, stones and elm trees and small quiet rivers and so on, and, of course, rustic people about."

J.R.R. TOLKIEN

Tolkien in Oxford, a BBC2 television documentary featuring an interview by John Izzard, 1968

J.R.R. TOLKIEN

The Shire was inspired by a few
square miles of countryside at Sarehole,
near Birmingham, that represented all that
Tolkien loved best about England.

"There was an old mill that really did grind corn, with two millers that I used for 'Farmer Giles of Ham', a great big pond with swans on it, a sandpit, a wonderful dell with flowers, a few old-fashioned village houses and a stream with another mill."

J.R.R. TOLKIEN
Interview with William Foster, "An Early History of the Hobbits",
Edinburgh Scotsman, 5 February 1972

Such was Tolkien's love of trees that in his Middle-earth, the hobbit calendar included a day initially known as "Tree's day" to give weekly homage to trees, later called "Trewsday", and finally Tuesday.

"I love trees, I don't know why. All my work is full of trees. ... I suppose ... in some simple-minded form of longing, I should have liked to have been able to make contact with a tree and find out what it feels about things."

J.R.R. TOLKIEN
Tolkien in Oxford, a BBC2 television documentary featuring
an interview with Tolkien by John Izzard, 1968

Tolkien belived that the sound of words could invoke meaning.

In *The Lord of the Rings*, Aragorn, Gandalf, Legolas and Gimli are approaching the Golden Hall of Rohan, when Aragorn chants a poem in Rohirric, "The Lament for the Rohirrimi", written for the ancient King of Eorl.

Legolas cannot understand the poem; however, he notes that the language is like the land of Rohan itself.

"That, I guess, is the language of the Rohirrim, for it is like to this land itself, rich and rolling in part, and else hard and stern as the mountains. But I cannot guess what it means, save that it is laden with the sadness of Mortal Men."

LEGOLAS

Commenting on "the Lament for the Rohirrimi"
in *The Two Towers*, 1954

J.R.R. TOLKIEN

As a philologist, Tolkien was
fascinated by names,
and found in them a starting point
and inspiration for stories.

"I always in writing, always start with a name. Give me a name and it produces a story."

J.R.R. TOLKIEN

BBC Radio 4 interview by Dennis Gerrolt, 26 November 1964

Name-making was key to
Middle-earth.

Tolkien devised an
extremely complex and
sophisticated scheme
of nomenclature
and linguistic history.

Place names were chosen with character and history in mind. So, the Shire names are in English, rather old-fashioned and remiscent of English country life, such as Nobottle, Bucklebury or Tuckborough.

The pubs have familiar and homely sounding names like "The Green Dragon", "The Ivy Bush" and "The Golden Perch".

In the summer of 1911, Tolkien set off with a heavy pack for a walking tour of the Swiss Alps.

Years later, he described his vivid memories of the trip in a letter to his son Michael, explaining how the landscape inspired the mountain settings of *The Hobbit*.

"I am ... delighted that you have made the acquaintance of Switzerland, and of the very part that I once knew best and which had the deepest effect on me. The hobbit's (Bilbo's) journey from Rivendale to the other side of the Misty Mountains, including the glissade down the slithering stones into the pine woods, is based on my adventures in 1911."

J.R.R. TOLKIEN
Letter to his son Michael, 1967, cited in M.S. Monsch, *Switzerland in Tolkien's Middle-earth*, 2021

Visitors to Switzerland can follow in Tolkien's footsteps by taking a Middle-earth tour to some of the breathtaking mountainous landscapes that inspired the stories.

At the Greisinger Museum in Jenins, visitors can see the dedicated Middle-earth collection, the largest and most important of its kind.

In Peter Jackson's film *The Desolation of Smaug*, the gold that Smaug has amassed is estimated to have a value of US$9.3 billion, according to Forbes.

Forests, such as The Old Forest,
Mirkwood, Fangorn and Lothlórien,
and individual trees, like the hobbits'
Party Trees or Old Man Willow,
are unique protagonists in Tolkien's
Middle-earth.

"In all my works, I take the part of trees as against all their enemies. Lothlórien is beautiful because there the trees were loved ... The Old Forest was hostile to two-legged creatures because of the memory of many injuries. Fangorn Forest was old and beautiful, but at the time of the story tense with hostility because it was threatened by a machine-loving enemy..."

J.R.R. TOLKIEN

"Letter to the Editor", *The Daily Telegraph*, 20 June 1972

Alongside the gloominess and evil present in Tolkien's stories, there are lighthearted moments, and 'the laughing folk, the little people', as Treebeard describes them, figure strongly in these.

"**G**andalf: Evil things do not come into this valley; but all the same we should not name them. The Lord of the Ring is not Frodo, but the master of the Dark Tower of Mordor, whose power is again stretching out over the world! We are sitting in a fortress. Outside it is getting dark.

Pippin: Gandalf has been saying many cheerful things like that."

THE FELLOWSHIP OF THE RING, 1954

Pippin's tongue-in-cheek remark to Frodo
when he joins his friends' conversation at Elrond's place
(the "Last Homely House") in Rivendell

The Book of Lost Tales comprises some of Tolkien's early stories, started as early as 1916 and published by his son Christopher in 1983–84. Embedded in English legend, the tales tell of the great westward voyage of a mortal man named Eriel to the Elvish Isle of Tol Eressëa, where he learns about the Elves' history.

The stories show the beginning of some of the legends that became part of *The Simarillion* and others that did not, such as "The Cottage of Lost Play". The passage opposite describes how, after a long and solitary journey, Eriel happens upon the cottage.

"**A** little down the western slope of the hill, his eye was arrested by a tiny dwelling whose many small windows were curtained snugly, yet only so that a most warm and delicious light, as of hearts content within, looked forth."

THE BOOK OF LOST TALES, 1983

Tolkien had a fondness for riddles. He drew from the traditions of old English verbal folklore where, such as in *The Hobbit*, the underdog almost always wins.

Bilbo is invisible to the dragon Smaug, but Smaug can smell him and demands to know his name. Not wanting to reveal his identity directly, or risk angering the dragon with a flat refusal, Bilbo responds with a riddle.

What dragon can resist the fascination of a riddle?

"I come from under the hill, and under the hills and over the hills my paths led. And through the air. I am he that walks unseen ... I am the clue-finder, the web-cutter, the stinging fly. I was chosen for the lucky number ... I am he that buries his friends alive and drowns them and draws them alive again from the water."

BILBO BAGGINS

Bilbo's riddle for Smaug when the dragon asks for his name, *The Hobbit*, 1937

Tolkien defines fairy stories as those that take place in *Faërie*, an enchanted realm that may or may not include fairies as characters.

He equates fairy stories, or fantasy, with imagination, and argues that it gives the reader a fresh perspective on their own world, as well as offering an escapist pleasure, in the same way as a prisoner who steps outside the prison walls.

"**F**aërie contains many things besides elves and fays, and besides dwarfs, witches, trolls, giants, or dragons; it holds the seas, the sun, the moon, the sky; and the earth, and all things that are in it: tree and bird, water and stone, wine and bread, and ourselves, mortal men, when we are enchanted."

J.R.R. TOLKIEN

Andrew Lang lecture at the University of St Andrews
on 8 March 1939, subsequently published as an essay in
The Monsters and the Critics and Other Essays, 1983

The Lord of the Rings includes its own fairy tale of the immortal Elf-maiden who weds a mortal man – "The Tale of Aragorn and Arwen". It mirrors the tale of Beren and Lúthien in *The Silmarillion*, set in an earlier age of Middle-earth.

"The Tale of Aragorn and Arwen is a tale about enduring love, triumphing over seemingly impossible odds, and sealed with Arwen's sacrifice of her Elven immortality in order to live with her human husband for 'six score years of great glory and bliss'."

WILLIAM GRAY

From *J.R.R. Tolkien and the Love of Faery. Fantasy, Myth and the Measure of Truth: Tales of Pullman, Lewis, Tolkien, MacDonald and Hoffmann,* 2009

The courage of the heroes in Tolkien's stories is inspired by the Norse legend of Ragnarök, in which the gods know that they are doomed in their final battle, but fight nonetheless.

In Middle-earth, the humble hobbits, without any special powers to speak of, face up to the proud and powerful Sauron.

"I've found it is the small things, everyday deeds of ordinary folk that keeps the darkness at bay. Simple acts of kindness and love. Why Bilbo Baggins? Perhaps it is because I am afraid and he gives me courage."

GANDALF

Explaining why he has chosen Bilbo for the quest,
The Hobbit, An Unexpected Journey
(dir. Peter Jackson, 2012), film based on Tolkien's novel
The Hobbit, 1937

Tolkien's dragons in Middle-earth are closely based on dragons from European legend: Fàfnir from Germanic mythology, the *Beowulf* dragon, and the dragon from the legend of Saint George.

They are equally referred to as serpents, great worms or drakes.

"I desired dragons with a profound desire. Of course, I in my timid body did not wish to have them in the neighbourhood, intruding into my relatively safe world, in which it was, for instance, possible to read stories in peace of mind, free from fear. But the world that contained even the imagination of Fàfnir was richer and more beautiful, at whatever cost of peril."

J.R.R. TOLKIEN

Andrew Lang lecture at the University of St Andrews on 8 March 1939, subsequently published as an essay in *The Monsters and the Critics and other essays*, 1983

Tolkien's stories often feature close and loving male friendships.

They call to mind the deep bonds the author himself formed throughout his life, whether it was with the fellow members of his schooldays club called the Tea Club, Barrovian Society (TCBS), or his friendships with fellow academics such as Eric Gordon or C.S. Lewis, or with the writers in his Oxford literary club, the Inklings.

"**Gimli:** Never thought I'd die fighting side by side with an Elf.

Legolas: What about side by side with a friend?

Gimli: Aye. I could do that."

Gimli, the dwarf, and Legolas, the elf fight together in the final battle with the armies of Mordor, *The Return of the King* (dir. Peter Jackson, 2003), film based on J.R.R. Tolkien's novel *The Lord of the Rings*.

CHAPTER
FIVE
Ents and Elves

For his creatures, Tolkien drew inspiration from fairy stories, from folklore, and from the Norse and Germanic mythology he so loved. He took elves, dwarves, wizards and dragons and made them his own.

Others, like the hobbits, the ents and the orcs, he essentially invented. In the rich world he constructed, each had a place, history, culture, language, legend and family tree.

Once a hobbit himself, the cave-dwelling Gollum was originally known as Sméagol. After being corrupted by the One Ring, he was named for his habit of making a horrible swallowing noise in his throat.

Gollum called the ring
"my precious", a term used
in Tolkien's time to express
affection for a loved one.

Throughout the stories,
he is torn between his lust
for the ring and his desire
to be free of it.

J.R.R. TOLKIEN

The names of Tolkien's characters are a story in their own right. Their influences include ancient languages, foreign languages and Tolkien's invented languages, but they inevitably paint a picture of their bearer and their place in the history of Middle-earth.

Frodo: in Old English, *frōd* means "wise".

Legolas: a Wood-elf form of the Sindarin word for "greenleaf".

Gríma Wormtongue (the spectre who haunts King Théoden and whispers false counsel to him). *Gríma* means "mask", "helmet" or "spectre" in Old English or Icelandic.

Gandálfr: taken from an Old Norse text, it roughly translates as "staff-elf".

Shelob: The name of the giant spider mixes the modern English pronoun "she" with the Middle English spelling of Old English *lobbe* ("spider").

Orcs are a brutish and evil race of human-shaped monsters, best known as servants and warriors for the Dark Lords of Middle-earth. It is suggested in *The Silmarillion* that they were elves kidnapped by the Dark Lord Melkor, who turned them into orcs.

Uruk-hai, were a type of orc bred by Saruman in the Third Age in order to create a stronger army for Sauron.

"**T**his is no rabble of mindless orcs. These are Uruk-hai. Their armour is thick and their shields broad."

GIMLI

Warning to the Rohirrim that Saruman is bringing a powerful army of Uruk-hai before the Battle of Helm's Deep, *The Two Towers* (dir. Peter Jackson, 2002), film adaptation of the Tolkien novel of the same name

The average life expectancy for a hobbit is 100 years. However, Gollum is estimated to have been born in the year TA 2430, and died on 25 March 3019, which would make him 589 years old when he died.

Such a long life was only possible because he possessed the One Ring.

In Middle-earth, trolls are vicious monsters of limited intelligence who live in the Misty Mountains and in Mordor.

Fortunately, most turn to stone when exposed to sunlight, which is their most vulnerable point.

There are seven types of troll:

Cave-trolls • Hill-trolls
Mountain-trolls • Olog-hai
Snow-trolls • Stone-trolls
Half-trolls

In his stories, Tolkien popularized the elves and dwarves of ancient mythology.

His elves drew from Northern European mythologies, especially the god-like and human-sized Norse Ljósálfar.

His dwarves are inspired by the creatures of Germanic myths: dark and short, they are smiths and artisans.

Tolkien's Gandalf calls to mind the Norse god Odin, with his long white beard, wide brimmed hat, staff and cloak.

TRAGIC CHARACTERS
IN MIDDLE-EARTH

Tolkien's stories tell of courage, love and friendship, but many of his characters are struck by tragedy or loss.

Gollum • Boromir
Arwen • Frodo Baggins
Thorin • Fili and Kili
Theoden • Haldir
Thranduil and Elrond's wives
Denethor

"**I** am glad you are here with me. Here at the end of all things, Sam."

FRODO

Frodo's words to Samwise as they prepare to die together on the slopes of Mount Doom, *The Return of the King*, 1955

Tolkien's Great Eagles are inspired by Norse and Icelandic mythology.

An ancient and sapient race, they are described as the greatest of all birds; proud, strong and noble-hearted.

Tolkien's early writings distinguish the eagles from other birds. He explains that the World (Eä) was bounded by the Walls of Night, and the space above the Earth up to the Walls was divided into three regions.

While common birds could only fly in the lower layer, the Eagles of Manwë, could fly "beyond the lights of heaven to the edge of darkness".

THE LOST ROAD AND OTHER WRITINGS, 1987

Tolkien's hobbits are far from obvious heroes. They are not physically powerful, or big – at two to four feet tall (60–120cm), they are even shorter than dwarves.

Gentle and peace-loving, they are happiest in an armchair by the fire with a meal on the stove.

The hobbits' bare, furry feet with leathery soles are their most singular trait, and one that is central to the plot in *The Hobbit*.

The dwarves choose Bilbo Baggins as their burglar because he can move with great stealth.

In *The Hobbit*, Thorin Oakenshield is
fatally wounded on the battlefield.
He bids farewell to Bilbo Baggins, asking
the hobbit for forgiveness – his greed
nearly cost him their friendship.

"There is more in you of good than you know, child of the kindly West. Some courage and some wisdom, blended in measure. If more of us valued food and cheer and song above hoarded gold, it would be a merrier world."

THORIN OAKENSHIELD

His farewell to Bilbo Baggins, *The Hobbit*, 1937

The hobbits – Bilbo Baggins, Frodo,
Sam, Merry and Pippin – are certainly
unlikely heroes at the outset,
but in the face of the worst possible
imaginable dangers, they struggle ahead,
to eventually win through.

Tolkien noted that this was not
unlike life.

"The hobbits are just rustic English people, made small in size because it reflects the generally small reach of their imagination – not the small reach of their courage or latent power ... But that seems ... like an allegory of the human race. I've always been impressed that we're here surviving because of the indomitable courage of quite small people against impossible odds: jungles, volcanoes, wild beasts, they struggle on, almost blindly in a way."

J.R.R. TOLKIEN
BBC Radio 4 interview by Dennis Gerrolt,
26 November 1964

J.R.R. TOLKIEN

Treebeard is the ultimate expression of Tolkien's love and respect for trees.

He is an ent or "tree herder", an ancient and majestic walking, talking tree, who is charged with defending the dwindling forests in Middle-earth. He expresses his wise ideas infuriatingly slowly.

"**Y**ou must understand, young Hobbit, it takes a long time to say anything in Old Entish. And we never say anything unless it is worth taking a long time to say."

TREEBEARD

His response to Merry and Pippin as they try to
convince him to lead the ents to war against the evil Saruman,
The Two Towers (dir. Peter Jackson, 2002), film adaptation
of the Tolkien novel of the same name

BEST-LOVED CHARACTERS IN
THE LORD OF THE RINGS

Whether it's an unassuming hero or the villain you love to hate, everyone has their favourite.

Aragorn

Legolas

Gandalf

Gollum

Samwise Gamgee

Gimli

Frodo Baggins

Pippin & Merry

Éowyn

Saruman

INNOVATION IN THE FILM SERIES

Duplicate, larger-scale film sets were used for the hobbits and dwarves, as they are shorter than the other races.

Gollum, the trolls and the ents were brought to life by CGI wizardry.

The films required 1,800 pairs of hobbit feet, 48,000 pieces of armour and 19,000 costumes.

POWERFUL WOMEN IN MIDDLE-EARTH

Of the relatively few women characters
in Middle-earth, some are incredibly powerful.

Éowyn, shieldmaiden of Rohan

Galadriel, the Lady of Lothlórien

Varda, Queen of the Valar

Nienna, Lady of Mercy

Melian, Queen of Doriath

Lúthien Tinúviel

Arwen Evenstar

Idril Celebrindal

Niënor of Hithlum

Rosie Cotton, a hobbit of the Shire

"**A**nd I shall not be dark, but beautiful and terrible as the Morning and the Night! Fair as the Sea and the Sun and the Snow upon the Mountain! Dreadful as the Storm and the Lightning! Stronger than the foundations of the earth. All shall love me and despair!"

GALADRIEL

Her response when Frodo offers her the One Ring,
The Fellowship of the Ring, 1954

As the King's niece, Éowyn is born into privilege – but with it, come certain expectations of her.

What she most desires is freedom and to be able to choose her own path.

"**A** cage ... To stay behind bars, until use and old age accept them, and all chance of doing great deeds is gone beyond recall or desire."

ÉOWYN

On being asked what she most fears,
The Return of the King, 1955

Sam Gamgee, or Samwise, is the ultimate defender of the Shire, and represents freedom, peace and an ordinary life. The true hero of the quest, he follows orders through love and duty, rather than personal gain.

Tolkien believed this same loyalty characterized the common man in the trenches in the First and Second World Wars.

"**M**y 'Sam Gamgee' is indeed a reflexion of the English soldier, of the privates and batmen I knew in the 1914 War and recognized as so far superior to myself."

J.R.R. TOLKIEN

In a letter to H. Cotton Minchin of 16 April 1956, cited in
A Companion to J.R.R. Tolkien, ed. Stuart D. Lee, 2022

CHAPTER
SIX
Tolkien's Legacy

Whether it's the enormous number of his
books still sold today, his rich academic
achievements, the desire he opened up among
readers for secondary worlds and heroic
quests, or the jaw-dropping films inspired by
his worlds, Tolkien left behind an extraordinary
cultural, historical and social imprint.

Tolkien's work brought high fantasy to a new generation, inspiring writers everywhere.

Pick up a contemporary fantasy novel and you'll often find a quest or an artefact of power, an unlikely hero, elves and dwarves, orcs and goblins, dragons, monstrous spiders or the shadow of evil falling across a pastoral, peaceful world.

Tolkien died on 2 September 1973. However, his life's work was to continue. His son Christopher, who had followed in his father's footsteps as an Oxford scholar, dedicated his own career to editing and overseeing the publication of two dozen editions of his father's works.

In 1977, the long-awaited *The Silmarillion*, was published and between 1983 and 1996, the mammoth 12-volume *History of Middle-earth* series, which revealed Tolkien's creative process.

Tolkien's most iconic maps were the three he produced for *The Lord of the Rings*: the main, small-scale map of Middle-earth and the larger-scale maps of the Shire and of Gondor and Mordor.

He and Christopher worked through the night to get every last detail in place before the publication deadline.

"I had to devote many days, the last three virtually without food or bed, to drawing, re-scaling and adjusting a large map, at which [Christopher] then worked for 24 hours (6am to 6am without bed) in re-drawing just in time."

J.R.R. TOLKIEN

Cited in Catherine McIlwaine, ed.,
Tolkien: Maker of Middle-earth, 2018

J.R.R. TOLKIEN

In his stories, Tolkien shares many
pearls of wisdom, often conveying big
ideas in a simple turn of phrase and
to great effect.

"**A** man that flies from his fear may find that he has only taken a short cut to meet it."

CHILDREN OF HÚRIN, 2007

Tolkien never wrote an autobiography.

However, he was a prolific letter writer, and a carefully curated collection of 354 of the hundreds of thoughtful epistles he penned over his lifetime are just as revealing.

The Letters of J.R.R. Tolkien (1981)
include love letters to his fiancée
during the war, words of advice for
his children, and countless letters
regarding his work to publishers,
colleagues, fans and critics.

J.R.R. TOLKIEN

8 EPIC BOARD GAMES INSPIRED BY *THE LORD OF THE RINGS*

The Lord of the Rings: The Card Game

War of the Ring

The Lord of the Rings: Journeys in Middle-earth

Hunt for the Ring

The Lord of the Rings

Middle-earth Strategy Battle Game

The Lord of the Rings: The Confrontation

Risk: The Lord of the Rings

There were some early attempts to bring Tolkien's world to the screen, not least that of The Beatles – also big Middle-earth fans.

Their own film adaptation of *The Lord of the Rings* would apparently have starred Paul McCartney as Frodo, John Lennon as Gollum, George Harrison as Gandalf and Ringo Starr as Sam!

Nobody expected Peter Jackson's film adaptations of *The Lord of the Rings* (produced by New Line Cinema) to be any good, given the enormity of the challenge. In fact, they were a bigger success than anyone could have imagined.

In 2003, Peter Jackson's
The Return of the King alone won:

11 Academy Awards,
tying with *Titanic* and *Ben-Hur*

5 BAFTAs, 3 Empire Awards,
4 Golden Globes, 1 Satellite Award
and 8 Saturn Awards

258 awards from 337 nominations

Tolkien fans can travel to New Zealand and take a once-in-a-lifetime journey through Middle-earth.

The trips go from Auckland to Queenstown and take in all the legendary landscapes of Sir Peter Jackson's film locations: soaring mountains, temperate rainforests and secluded river valleys.

El Senyor dels Anells, Der Herr der Ringe, Hringadróttinssaga...

Translating *The Lord of the Rings* will have been no easy feat for its more than 50 translators. Aside from the sheer volume – a massive 1,178 pages in the English version – it presents difficulties such as the complex interplay between English and Elvish nomenclature in the book or the proper names in Old English and Old Norse.

FAMOUS TOLKIEN FANS

Queen Margrethe II of Denmark
(illustrator of Tolkien's work)

Barack Obama

Prince Charles and Prince William

Árpád Göncz (former president of Hungary
and Hungarian translator of Tolkien's work)

The Beatles

James Cameron

Isaac Asimov

Fernando Torres (has a tattoo of
his name in Tengwar)

In the New Year Honours of 1 January 1972, Queen Elizabeth appointed J.R.R. Tolkien a Commander of the Order of the British Empire "For services to English Literature".

Tolkien describes *eucatastrophe* as a sudden happy turn in a story that "pierces you with a joy that brings tears".

This mingling of profound joy and grief is present in *The Return of the the King*, when the heroes gather to celebrate the victory, and a ministrel sings.

"**A**nd all the host laughed and wept, and in the midst of their merriment and tears the clear voice of the minstrel rose like silver and gold ... And he sang to them, now in the Elven-tongue, now in the speech of the West, until their hearts, wounded with sweet words, overflowed, and their joy was like swords..."

THE RETURN OF THE KING, 1955

In 2022, Tolkien's world returned in an epic-scale production for the small screen, *The Lord of the Rings: The Rings of Power*.

Produced by Amazon Studios in cooperation with the Tolkien Estate and Trust, HarperCollins and New Line Cinema, the five-season drama draws heavily from *The Silmarillion*.

Also filmed in the majestic landscapes of New Zealand, *The Rings of Power* begins the tale in a period of relative peace and covers all the major events of Middle-earth's Second Age: the forging of the Rings of Power, the rise of the Dark Lord Sauron, the fall of Númenor and the last alliance between elves and men.

J.R.R. TOLKIEN

After Edith's death in 1971,
Tolkien returned to Oxford, the city
he loved.

He died in 1973 at the age of 81.

At a memorial service, his poignant
short story *Leaf by Niggle* was
read – he surely would not have
been displeased.

"**B**efore him stood the Tree, his Tree, finished. If you could say that of a Tree that was alive, its leaves opening, its branches growing and bending in the wind that Niggle had so often felt and guessed, and had so often failed to catch. He gazed at the Tree, and slowly he lifted his arms and opened them wide. 'It's a gift!' he said."

LEAF BY NIDDLE, 1945

Every year on 3 January,
the Tolkien Society
invites fans all over the
world to mark the
author's birthday with a
simple toast.

At 9pm your local
time, wherever you are,
raise a glass to the
much-loved author.
Simply:
"The Professor!"